GOD
IS
WITH YOU

SWAMI MUKTANANDA

Published by SYDA Foundation
371 Brickman Rd., PO Box 600, South Fallsburg, NY 12779, USA

Design by Derek Beecham
Cover illustration by Joël Langlois

First published 1978. Second edition, 1993

Printed in the United States of America

07 06 05 04 03 02 01 00 99 98   5 4 3 2

ISBN 0-911307-72-9

GOD
IS
WITH YOU

SWAMI MUKTANANDA

A SIDDHA YOGA MEDITATION PUBLICATION
PUBLISHED BY SYDA FOUNDATION

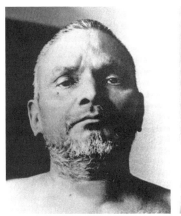

Bhagawan Nityananda　　　*Swami Muktananda*

SWAMI MUKTANANDA
and the Lineage of Siddha Yoga Meditation Masters

Swami Muktananda was born in 1908 to a family of prosperous landowners near the South Indian city of Mangalore. Around the age of fifteen he met the renowned saint Bhagawan Nityananda, whom he would later recognize as his spiritual Master. Within six months of this encounter, the boy set out from home in search of the direct experience of God, a journey that would ultimately last almost a quarter of a century and take him three times across the length and breadth of India. He met his first teacher, Siddharudha Swami, who was one of the renowned scholars and saints of that time, in an ashram in Hubli, two hundred miles to the north of his parents' home. It was there that he studied Vedanta, took the vows of *sannyasa*, or monkhood, and received the name Swami Muktananda, "the bliss of liberation."

When Siddharudha died in 1929, Swami Muktananda began his pilgrimage to the holy sites of India. He met and learned from more than sixty saints, always looking for the one who would give him the experience of God. He searched for eighteen years, during which time Swami Muktananda mastered the major scriptures of India, received training in an array of disciplines and skills — from hatha yoga to cooking and Ayurvedic medicine — and still he did not find what he sought.

At last one of the saints he met sent him to Bhagawan Nityananda, the Siddha Master (perfected spiritual teacher) he had seen so many years before. Bhagawan Nityananda was then living in the hamlet of Ganeshpuri, fifty miles northeast of Bombay. Recognizing Bhagawan Nityananda as the Guru he had been seeking, Swami Muktananda later said that this meeting ended his wandering forever. From Bhagawan Nityananda he received shaktipat, the sacred initiation of the Siddhas by which one's inner spiritual energy is awakened. This energy, known in yoga as *kundalini*, is a divine potential that exists within each human being; once awakened, it enables a seeker to reach the most sublime levels of inner experience.

With this initiation, Swami Muktananda became a disciple, dedicating himself to the spiritual path set forth by his Guru. Thus began nine years of intense transformation, during which Muktananda fully explored the inner realms of consciousness through meditation and finally became steady in his experience of the fullness and ecstasy of the inner Self. In 1956, Bhagawan Nityananda declared that his disciple's inner journey was complete: Swami Muktananda had attained Self-realization, the unchanging experience of union with God.

Even after he had achieved the goal of his discipleship, Swami Muktananda remained a devoted disciple, continuing to live quietly near Ganeshpuri. Bhagawan Nityananda established him in a small ashram of his own, and for five years Guru and disciple lived less than a mile from each other. Then in 1961, just before his death, Bhagawan Nityananda passed on to Swami Muktananda the grace-bestowing power of the Siddha Masters, investing him with the capacity to give spiritual awakening, or shaktipat, to others. On that day Bhagawan Nityananda told him, "The entire world will see you."

In the decades that followed, Baba Muktananda traveled throughout India and, later, the rest of the world. During the course of three international tours, Baba imparted to others the same shaktipat initiation he himself had received, and he also introduced seekers to the practices and philosophy of the spiritual path he called Siddha Yoga meditation. People who had never before heard of meditation found that in Baba Muktananda's presence they were drawn into a stillness within that gave their lives new focus and meaning. He introduced programs to give shaktipat initiation to large groups and explained to people the ongoing process of transformation that was unfolding within them.

In 1982, shortly before his death, Swami Muktananda designated his successor, Swami Chidvilasananda. She had been his disciple since early childhood and had traveled with him since 1973, translating into English his writings, his lectures, and the many informal exchanges he had with his devotees. She was an advanced spiritual seeker with a great longing for God, and she became an exemplary disciple. She was guided in her sadhana by her Guru, who meticulously prepared her to succeed him as Guru. In early May of 1982, Swami Chidvilasananda took formal vows of monkhood, and later that month Swami Muktananda bequeathed to her the power and authority of the Siddha Yoga lineage, the same spiritual legacy that his Guru had passed on to him. Since that time, Gurumayi, as she is widely known, has given shaktipat and taught the Siddha Yoga meditation practices to seekers in many countries, introducing them to Swami Muktananda's message:

Meditate on your Self.
Honor your Self.
Worship your Self.
Understand your own Self.
God dwells within you as you.

Gurumayi Chidvilasananda

God is nothing but supreme bliss.
He dwells within you
as much as He dwells within Himself.

Everything that you see in this world
has come from God
and eventually merges back into Him.

God is supremely independent.
He is faultless, taintless,
and absolutely pure.
He is complete within Himself.
He pervades everywhere.

He is *sat chit ānanda*.

Sat means the Truth;
the Truth that exists all the time,
in all places, in all things.

Chit is Consciousness.
It is the power of seeing in sight.
It is the power of tasting in taste.
It is the power of feeling in touch.

It illumines what exists
and what does not exist.
Dwelling in all objects, *chit* illuminates them.

Ānanda is pure bliss.
God's bliss keeps surging and increasing
all the time.

Ānanda is the independent joy
that you experience within yourself.
For the sake of that joy,
you spend your life seeking bliss outside.

There are many people in the world,
yet God is only one.
There are many paths, many religions,
yet God is only one.
He is not many.

People describe Him in many different ways.
He is Krishna, Shiva, Allah,
and the Void.

Because of their different temperaments,
people follow different paths to God.
However, God is within.
He is perceived through meditation
and knowledge.

People follow different paths
because of their different temperaments.
But they reach Him alone,
just as rivers reach the ocean.

God is the Master of the universe;
He pervades everything outside us
and He is inside too.

God doesn't live apart from us
somewhere else.
God dwells within.
It is God who exists in this human form.

O God,
what a wonder!
After creating all these human beings,
You entered into them to live there.

An ecstatic being exclaimed,
"I saw God in myself."

He also said,
"You may break a temple,
you may break a mosque,
you may break the sacred shrines
of Ka'ba and Kibla.
But never break anybody's heart
because God, the Master, dwells there."

The heart is the true temple of God.

Since a temple was built,
God never lived in it.
Since the heart was created,
God never left it.

People hate others.
People slander others.
People insult others. People hurt others.
Then they try to worship God
in a church or temple.
Isn't this an insult to God?
They reject Consciousness
and worship only matter.

The true worship of God is to respect all,
because God dwells in everyone's heart.

Inside the heart lies supreme light.
It is the effulgence of God.

Once you start perceiving
this inner light,
you will see it everywhere,
as everything is filled with that light.

The light that you see around you
is not truly light.
Compared to the real light,
it is nothing but darkness.

This entire world exists in God's light.
It scintillates and shimmers everywhere:
in front of you, behind you, within you.

You should see the inner light
at least once.

Due to ignorance,
you have considered yourself
an individual soul
and the world a mere world.
The moment you become aware of God
within yourself,
then this world becomes paradise.

Never believe that God is opposed
to your worldly life.

When you look at a beautiful form
and you become wonder struck,
that is the wonder of the form of God.
When you listen to a beautiful sound
and you become still,
that stillness is the sound of God.
When you meet a friend and embrace him
and you stop for a moment out of joy,
that is the perfect peace of God.

Don't think you have to turn away
from all these things.
The experience of God is in them too.

To see God in everything
as well as oneself
is the greatest knowledge,
greatest meditation, greatest religion,
and the highest path to God.

You only experience fear
when you don't take refuge in God
and are distant from God.
If you have complete faith in Him,
then you have no fear.

When you experience
the all-pervasiveness of God,
then your fear is annihilated.
What is there left to fear?

As a river merges into the ocean
and becomes the ocean,
one day you will merge
into the ocean of God's bliss.

The more we forget ourselves,
the more we understand of God.

Lose yourself in Him.

Forget your past actions.
Don't think of future actions.
Live in this very moment.
Keep repeating: I am He;
He is inside me; I am inside Him.

It is not very hard to attain God,
as you have already attained Him.

Only your understanding tells you
you haven't.

To attain the Self is the highest good.

If after attaining this human body
one doesn't see the inner Self,
what greater misfortune can there
be than this?

Understand, you are God.

Remember,
whether you understand it or not,
God is within you.

Don't ever forget this understanding:
Even if you forget God,
God doesn't forget you even for a moment.

FURTHER READING

Published by SYDA Foundation

SWAMI MUKTANANDA

Play of Consciousness
From the Finite to the Infinite
Where Are You Going?
Kundalini
Conversations with Swami Muktananda
Nothing Exists That Is Not Shiva
Bhagawan Nityananda of Ganeshpuri
Mukteshwari
I Have Become Alive
I Am That
The Perfect Relationship
Meditate
Secret of the Siddhas
Does Death Really Exist?
Selected Essays
Reflections of the Self
Mystery of the Mind
Light on the Path

GURUMAYI CHIDVILASANANDA

Remembrance
Enthusiasm
The Yoga of Discipline
Kindle My Heart
Inner Treasures
My Lord Loves a Pure Heart
Ashes at My Guru's Feet
The Magic of the Heart

You may learn more about the teachings
and practices of Siddha Yoga meditation by contacting

SYDA FOUNDATION   *or*   GURUDEV SIDDHA PEETH
PO Box 600, 371 Brickman Rd.   PO Ganeshpuri, PIN 401 206
South Fallsburg, NY 12779-0600,   District Thana, Maharashtra,
USA   India
Tel: (914) 434-2000

Please visit our website at www.siddhayoga.org

For further information on books in print by Swami Muktananda and
Swami Chidvilasananda, editions in translation, and audio and
video recordings, please contact

SIDDHA YOGA MEDITATION BOOKSTORE
PO Box 600, 371 Brickman Rd
South Fallsburg, NY 12779-0600, USA
Tel: (914) 434-2000 ext. 1700

Call toll-free from the United States and Canada: 888-422-3334
Fax toll-free from the United States and Canada: 888-422-3339